T0272748

L.E.C.H.E

1) Genesis

THE HUMAN RACE
The genesis of every architectural project goes hand in hand with an understanding of the **human race** through our lived experience.

PRIVATE PUBLIC
Every individual faces life as an **independent** being. However it would be wrong and unnatural to think that there isn't, as already mentioned, a conscious unchangeable trait that links us all, over which control becomes complicated. The desire to have a safe private place together with the innate need to feel at ease within society have made both **public and private** architecture indispensable.

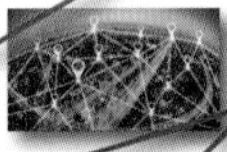

GEOGRAPHICAL CO
Complex human agg
functional and social
improve and evolve.
to the community ar
find inspiration from
environmentally-friend

HOSTILE NATURE
Imagine, just for a moment, what our ancestors must have felt before **hostile inhospitable nature**, caught in a **terrible storm with thunder and lightning streaking across the sky**, phenomena that still frighten us today and disturb our peace even within the protected comfort of our homes.

GLOBAL WARMING
For this reason, it is of the utmost **importance** not to sideline the irreversible problem of **global warming** and the innumerable alternative solutions to **fossil fuels**.

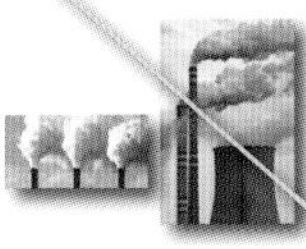

HARMONY
Although it might seem banal and universally known, I think any consideration of architecture and its practice must start from these simple concrete points, realizing the extent of our unconscious **desire for protection** and the need to **live in harmony** and **balance** in **"shelters"** that are part of our known context.

ECOSUSTAINABLE MATERIALS
Building products are of great importance. Much care must be given to the very many so called natural or "eco-sustainable" **materials** available, efficient in terms of energy, but not wholly sustainable on account of the environmentally harmful way they are processed, used and disposed of. Solutions exist today, however, that make any type of excuse or alibi unacceptable.

CITIES
Jumping a few millennia and the constant improvements in building systems that have become increasingly complex and involved, we have to admire the urban conglomeration we call **cities** as we look back at the history of our evolution.

INTEGRATED FORMS
Even if the use of appropriate materials and building systems is very important, even more important is placing our architectures in the landscape and urban fabric in a logical and appropriate manner, trying to create **forms and volumes** that are intrinsically able to forego the need for artificial **heating and cooling** systems.

ARCHITECTURE
It was only thanks to our in
and improve our wellbeing
our heads", unconsciously
Architecture.

SHELTERS
Our first shelters – **grottos in caves** – overcame the irrationality of these events with the rationality afforded by a **safe and comfortable shelter**. This was our first perception of space as a volume, a hollow inside a naturally constructed mass, known as the Earth's crust, the result of primordial stratifications and tectonic movements.

GREEN POLICIES
Fortunately the great powers, although not all of them, are promoting **green policies**, making these compulsory political and legal norms. The Earth's inhabitants are also rapidly gaining awareness, changing positively. As a knowledgeable person, the architect and his work must find efficient solutions for environmental sustainability, and our dramatic energy insufficiency, raising awareness of the severity of the problem. Sustainability **does not stop** at mere ecological aspects, which fail to take into account the economic and social features of our contemporary world.

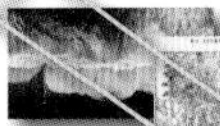

THE IRRATIONAL
The genesis of our existence, i.e. survival, depends also on the **irrational**. It was because of the world's irrationality caused by a lack of understanding of what surrounded them that our ancestors started protecting themselves against unknown actions, like the elements, learning to survive in a hostile **irrational** world.

BLADE

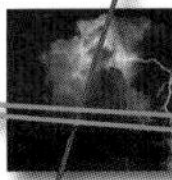

EVOLUTION
Our training experience must be **an ongoing activity** if we are to remain attuned to the real world. Partnerships with specialists are vital to understanding the variables involved. This is vital when forming a **project team**

A CLEAR MENTAL VISION
All concerned must have a clear understanding of the **mental vision** behind the project. This includes not only designers and construction companies but also the future occupants, who should take on board and share the significance and meaning of the architecture. Sustainability and design concept must never clash.

SUSTAINABILITY
If understood as a practical tangible feature, **sustainability** is not just about ecology, as is generally thought, but includes aspects that have to do with the construction, the landscape, and political, historical, economic, and social concerns. There will be points on which even the most environmentally committed client will not be in agreement. Mediation on economic and commercial questions is needed if feasible practicable design projects and constructions are to be achieved. Much is expected of the architect in terms of design and final outcome, but the result is often tangible proof that not always can all aspects be fully respected.

TRANSFORM TO IMPROVE
Defining a project "concept" as a function of the **existing landscape** not only prompts ideas and solutions but also helps our mental and creative processes grasp the special features of the place, helping us identify the most suitable approach for the particular project built for a precise function and client at that particular moment in time. The process guiding an architect, from the conceptual to the building stage **must be to improve the landscape through transformation**, understanding and highlighting its positive features and reducing its negative aspects. The underlying concept must be clear from the outset through the various phases from design through to construction if we are to make logical rational use of architecture.

CONCEPT AND FORM
The concept should not only be about form, devised as a self-referential exercise, but rather solve innumerable complexities. The process of bringing a building into existence involves many minds and specialists able to understand and interpret the social, economic, urban, and landscape aspects of a brief.

WORKSITE AND THEORY
These two different yet complementary aspects of making architecture are the basis of my own experience, one naturally following on from the other. Practice on the **worksite** led me to study past and present theory under great masters like **Kenneth Frampton, Steven Holl, and Elia Zenghelis. Construction, architecture, landscape, the natural environment and cities** all require in-depth understanding and can be viewed in terms of building processes and technologies. Importantly, for me the architectural concept and project must not only **be compatible** with the place but **also with the world of building**.

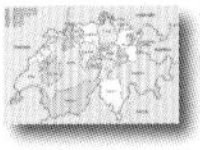

CANTON TICINO
My professional work thus far has been mainly in Switzerland's Italian speaking **Canton Ticino**; my projects showing great attention to the natural environment in which they are placed as well as to the individual concerned, whether client or final user.

BRICKLAYER
My first job in a worksite was as a **bricklayer**. This prompted me subsequently to become an architect. Commissions and requests to finalize the executive phases of creative activity led my firm to develop dozens of projects, giving us little time to take stock and participate in local, national, and especially international, competitions. Initially therefore we were engaged in residential briefs. This has allowed us to explore many different scales, get to know the market and understand the industrial and technological world linked to architecture.

THE 5 SENSES
Built architecture can be **seen, touched, heard, smelled, and lived in** everyday; it is made of **light, space, and matter**. Our senses are part of what we are and our daily lives. Each of us has memories and déjà vu of past experiences, both good and bad. They all entail a place, a space, and architecture. The architect must therefore develop **simple pragmatic** concepts for the good of man and his **habitat**, without, however, neglecting the construction and economic aspects that are integral to architecture.

ORCHESTRA
Today an architect is merely the **conductor of an orchestra**. Although an orchestra conductor cannot be expected to know how to play many different instruments individually or at the same time, he must, however, know the characteristics and prerogatives of each in order to make them produce the harmonious symphony that is architecture.

3) Concept

WELL-BEING
The architect's creativity must be focused on the **well-being of the landscape and the individual**, concerns that must never be antithetical, serving only personal needs or speculation.

PRÊT

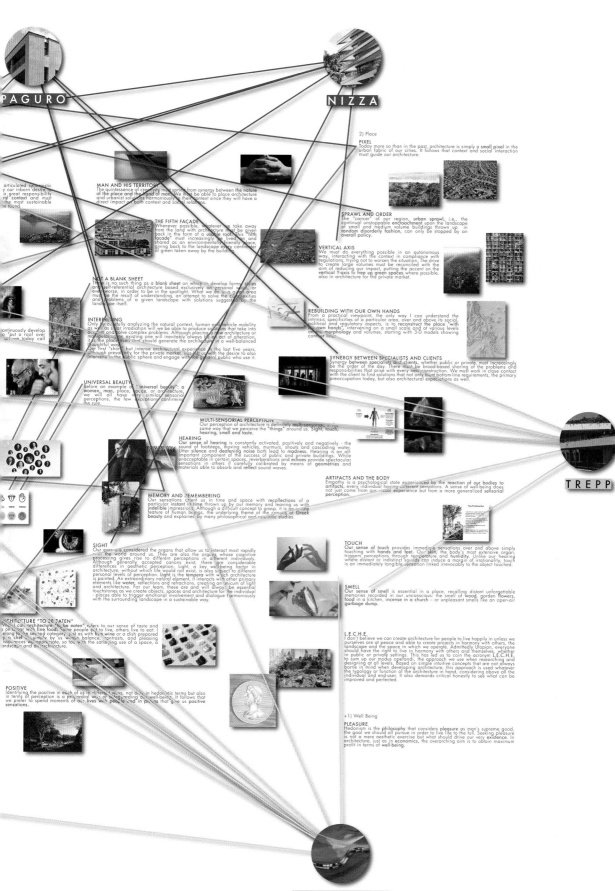

articulated synergistic
... our inborn desire...
... a great responsibility
...al context and must
...e found.

MAN AND HIS TERRITORY
The quintessence of creativity must spring from synergy between the nature of the place and the hand of man. We must be able to place architecture and urbanist solutions harmoniously in their context since they will have a direct impact on both context and social relations.

THE FIFTH FAÇADE
Whenever possible, whatever we take away from the land must be given back in the form of a usable roof. This "fifth façade" must increasingly be lived on and shared as an environmentally friendly place, giving back to the landscape every centimeter of green taken away by the building.

NOT A BLANK SHEET
There is no such thing as a blank sheet on which to develop forms, styles and self-referential architecture based exclusively on personal whims, or even worse, in order to be in the spotlight. What we do in a given area must be the result of understanding, an attempt to solve the complexities and problems of a given landscape with solutions suggested by the landscape itself.

INTERPLAYING
Only by carefully analyzing the natural context, human and vehicle mobility as well as solar irradiation will we be able to produce solutions that take into account and solve complex problems. Although placing a new architecture or manipulating an existing one will inevitably always be an act of alteration, it is the process itself that should generate the architecture in a well-balanced thoughtful way.
Our first "shot", but intense architectural experience in the last five years, although prevalently for the private market, fills us with the desire to also intervene in the public sphere and engage with the general public who use it.

UNIVERSAL BEAUTY
Before an example of "universal beauty": a woman, man, place, space, or architecture, we will all have very similar sensorial perceptions, the few exceptions confirming the rule.

MULTI-SENSORIAL PERCEPTION
Our perception of architecture is definitely multi-sensorial, in the same way that we perceive the "things" around us. Sight, touch, hearing, smell and taste.

HEARING
Our sense of hearing is constantly activated, positively and negatively - the sound of footsteps, moving vehicles, murmurs, shouts and cascading water. Utter silence and deafening noise both lead to madness. Hearing is an all-important component of the success of public and private buildings. While unacceptable in certain spaces, reverberations and echoes provide spectacular sensations in others if carefully calibrated by means of geometries and materials able to absorb and reflect sound waves.

MEMORY AND REMEMBERING
Our sensations orient us in time and space with recollections of a particular instant in time thrown up by our memory and leaving us with indelible impressions. Although a difficult concept to grasp, it is an innate feature of human beings, the underlying theme of the canons of Greek beauty and explained by many philosophical and scientific studies.

...continuously develop
...o "put a roof over
...ue we today call

SIGHT
Our eyes are considered the organs that allow us to interact most rapidly with the world around us. They are also the organs whose cognitive processing gives rise to different perceptions in different individuals. Although generally accepted canons exist, there are considerable differences in aesthetic perception. Light, a key well-being factor in architecture, without which life would not exist, is also subject to different personal levels of perception. Light is the tempera with which architecture is painted. An extraordinary natural element, it interacts with other primary elements like water, reflections and refractions, creating an "unicum of light and architecture. For our team, these are and will always be essential touchstones as we create objects, spaces and architecture for the individual - places able to trigger emotional involvement and dialogue harmoniously with the surrounding landscape in a sustainable way.

ARCHITECTURE "TO BE EATEN"
What can architecture "to be eaten" refers to our sense of taste and... on our way with fine food. Some people opt to live, others live to eat... ...belong to the second category, just as with fine wine or a dish prepared ... y a chef ... simply by us whose balance, contrasts, and pleasing ...ssquances we appreciate, so too with the satisfying use of a space, a ...andscape or an architecture.

POSITIVE
Identifying the positive in each of us in different ways, not only in hedonistic terms but also in terms of perception is a primordial way of safeguarding our well-being. It follows that we prefer to spend moments of our lives with people and in places that give us positive sensations.

2) Place

PIXEL
Today more so than in the past, architecture is simply a small pixel in the urban fabric of our cities. It follows that context and social interaction must guide our architecture.

SPRAWL AND ORDER
The "cancer" of our region, urban sprawl, i.e., the continual unstoppable encroachment upon the landscape of small and medium volume buildings thrown up in random disorderly fashion, can only be stopped by an overall policy.

VERTICAL AXIS
We must do everything possible in an autonomous way, interacting with the context in compliance with regulations, trying not to worsen the situation. The drive to create large volumes must be reconciled with the aim of reducing our impact, putting the accent on the vertical Y-axis to free up green spaces where possible, also in architecture for the private market.

REBUILDING WITH OUR OWN HANDS
From a practical viewpoint, the only way I can understand the intrinsic specificities of a particular area, over and above its social, political and regulatory aspects, is to reconstruct the place "with our own hands", intervening on a small scale and at various levels of their morphology and volumes, starting with 3-D models showing contour lines.

SYNERGY BETWEEN SPECIALISTS AND CLIENTS
Synergy between specialists and clients, whether public or private, must increasingly be the order of the day. There must be broad-based sharing of the problems and responsibilities that arise with every new construction. We must work in close contact with the client to find solutions that not only must bottom-line requirements, the primary preoccupation today, but also architectural expectations as well.

ARTIFACTS AND THE BODY
Empathy is a psychological state experienced by the reaction of our bodies to artifacts, every individual having different sensations. A sense of well-being does not just come from our visual experience but from a more generalized sensorial perception.

TOUCH
Our sense of touch provides immediate sensations over and above simply touching with hands and feet. Our skin, the body's most extensive organ, triggers perceptions through temperature and humidity. Unlike our hearing where distant or indistinct sounds can induce a margin of irrationality, touch is an immediately tangible sensation linked irrevocably to the object touched.

SMELL
Our sense of smell is essential in a place, recalling distant unforgettable memories recorded in our unconscious: the smell of wood, garden flowers, food in a kitchen, incense in a church – or unpleasant smells like an open-air garbage dump.

L.E.C.H.E.
I don't believe we can create architecture for people to live happily in unless we ourselves are at peace and able to create projects in harmony with others, the landscape and the space in which we operate. Admittedly Utopian, everyone should have the right to live in harmony with others and themselves, whether in public or private settings. This has led us to coin the acronym L.E.C.H.E. to sum up our modus operandi, the approach we use when researching and designing at all levels, based on simple intuitive concepts that are not always borne in mind when developing architecture, this approach is used whatever the typology or function of the architecture in hand, considering above all the individual and end-user. It also demands critical honesty to see what can be improved and perfected.

+1) Well Being

PLEASURE
Hedonism is the philosophy that considers pleasure as man's supreme good, the goal we should all pursue in order to live life to the full. Seeking pleasure is not a mere aesthetic exercise but what should drive our very existence. In architecture, just as in economics, the overarching aim is to obtain maximum profit in terms of well-being.

INDEX

ANALYSIS

1 GENESIS

2 PLACE

DESIGN

3 CONCEPT

CONSTRUCTION

+1 WELL-BEING

GOAL

The world as we know it today is increasingly fast-paced, complex and voluble. Even more than in the past, working within an increasingly dynamic interdisciplinary system able to embrace the inevitable advances and growing sector specialization has become indispensable. It implies constant self-assessment and an ability to look at a topic from many different angles – neither easy nor obvious when we are completely focused on a specific objective. But in-depth analysis of a problem will always reveal a range of complex aspects that cannot be handled by just one skill set.

'OPEN BEING' equates with a proactive mindset open to the many possible solutions a problem offers in an interdisciplinary environment.

Very often, serendipity reveals unexplored avenues, solutions we would never have thought of had we not been forced by narrow-minded dogmas to think outside the box. Pushing reasoning to its limit and approaching a question from a whole new perspective can confirm assumptions we had previously glimpsed looking at the other side of the coin. Indeed, it is only by sifting through the immensely valuable 'Obvious' that we can arrive at theoretical and practical ways of managing the wealth of information, or Big Data, now available. The Obvious is not necessarily banal when harnessed to talent and inspiration. The Obvious has the added advantage of being understood by everyone: in the case of architecture, from the initial concept through to the technical and practical features. The Obvious also simplifies complexity in the building phase, leading to time and cost savings.

This monograph presents a series of concepts, ideas and thoughts. It is the story of a journey: of our frenetic daily lives, always on the move but interspersed by moments of transition that prompt reflection. An architecture logbook noting how we have developed as a practice, it looks at how we have constantly extended our know-how with each built project. Neither a declaration of success, nor the announcement of a new start, this volume simply marks a milestone, a moment in which we pause to take stock.

These fragments, ideas and considerations could only have come together with the help of people and time – always in short supply. Mino Caggiula Architects was partnered in this effort by THE PLAN and Enrico Leonardo Fagone.

Fleeting thoughts – in color or black and white – accompany us every day as we go about our work. Sometimes they are short-lived, indistinct and confused. At others, they appear with clarity, inspiring and profound. This unconstrained mental space often takes us into distant places far removed from our original journey. Likewise, this book can be read in several ways: as a concise architectural overview, an account of meta-design concepts, a crescendo of increasingly meaningful images, or as an insightful analysis of architecture in the making.

1 Genesis   2 Place   3 Concept   +1 Well-being

These fragments have been divided into 3 categories +1 and sum up the essence of our *modus operandi* whose goal is continual improvement and growth. The first two categories focus on analysis and research, which then take shape in the architecture to be built. We seek to step outside exclusively anthropocentric contemporary architecture and achieve an interaction between man and his environment that leads to wellbeing, mitigating wherever possible the impact our many daily actions have on the world.

Mino Caggiula

GENESIS

THE INNATE PREMISES
OF CONTINUOUS
HUMAN EVOLUTION

1

"It is not the strongest of the species that survives, nor the most intelligent; it is the one most adaptable to change."

Charles Darwin (1809-1882)

ANTHROPOLOGY

The term 'genesis' sums up the set of inborn traits that have led to the evolution of the human race. They also lend meaning to architecture. The design process starts with studies and models of man's development as technology evolved to provide an in-depth analysis of needs and functions, which in turn is the basis for defining a new organizational framework for cities. It is a process that takes on board a dimension that must be part of how we conceive and realize new architecture today. **We believe that anthropology, or a broad understanding of man's needs as he undergoes continual evolution, has a precise meaning in the world of architecture. It implies a design process geared to man's evolving requirements that is never a self-referential, self-celebratory portrait of the architect but subordinate to the values inherent in each brief, whether a public or private commission.** Central to any preliminary analysis, initial concept and meta-design process is the individual, the collectivity and their relationship with the existing urban fabric or landscape. All-important therefore is the interface with the final user/client, and a program that is as compatible as possible with the particular context and constraints. Put more simply, every architectural project must start with a full understanding of how we human beings have lived and related to our context. Understanding how we have lived and survived requires not only taking into account the physical and rational but also the psychological and irrational. Our ancestors started by having to protect themselves from the vagaries of unknown forces like the weather, learning to survive in a hostile world. Our first shelters – grottos and caves – offset irrational events with the rationality of safe comfortable inhabitable spaces. Only by respecting the same innate ancestral prerequisites can we create architecture today able to dialogue with the contemporary world. We must never forget these primordial needs. They must be carried forward through the generations as we adapt to our continuously changing requirements.

Our first perception of a safe space was a hollow volume found in the naturally formed mass known as the Earth's crust, the result of countless tectonic movements and stratifications.

Stephens Gap Cave
Woodville, Alabama, United States of America

The firm's first project dealt with one of the most delicate and often controversial architectural topics: the extension of a pre-existing building, in this case, a non-listed townhouse in the city of Lugano in Switzerland's Italian-speaking canton. Historic buildings are frequent subjects of architectural briefs. The request is either for maintenance, adaptive reuse, but very often for partial or total rebuilding. As a rule, an architect's first brief is either a residential building from scratch in which he/she can express his/her own vision of consistent function and form, or a renovation and adaptive reuse commission, working within the constraints of what already exists. **The *Paguro* project had a dual requirement: renovation and extension. Our studio aimed to meld past and present, memory and future, and extend the reconciliation of old and new to a wider urban level.** The striking juxtaposition of the new and the – now renovated – existing construction is achieved through well-balanced compositional massing. The result is a fresh image: a building with different façades linked by rounded profiles on each side, forms that gave the building its name. **The 'Hermit Crab' does not seek to hide the evident differences between old and new, comfortably respecting the canons and linguistic codes of each.** This first brief was a useful exercise, signaling the perspective we were to adopt in subsequent projects. It refined an expressive language that eschews in-your-face designer-architecture effects in favor of a more thoughtful concept, a deeper reflection on the value and meaning of building, through an operation within architecture, prior to design and construction.

Built in the early 20th Century, the original townhouse boasts handsome façades. The home for many years of an extended family, every corner of the house tells the story of the lives lived within its walls. Like all houses once lived in, it bore signs of former lives: faded wallpaper, carpeting impregnated with the dust from fireplaces burning during long winter nights or spread by the gentle streams of warm air from iron radiators. Although by then dark and gloomy, the house seemed to be silently waiting. The client, however, wanted something new. **At times though the designer takes his cue from words and inferences in conversations, in this case, with a client whose family had strong emotional ties with the house. Both demolition and extension were feasible solutions. But extension would simply have produced a copycat building, in other words, a fake.** This led us to explore an alternative to both demolition and extension: the juxtaposition of contrasting elements that together would make a compositional whole - the most difficult solution, demanding dialogue between different languages. This was when the metaphor of the 'hermit crab' came to mind in acknowledgement of the fact that growth and natural evolution inevitably mean change. A new shell was developed with a south-facing elevation with large apertures overlooking a quiet residential zone, and a more closed frontage on the west side giving onto the busy Via Zurigo. The building was 'sliced in two,' the link with the new volume defined by a straight line perfectly aligned on the north-south axis, the symbolic meeting point of past and present. Inside, floorplan and volume mutate effortlessly, passing from old to new, communal living areas now in the new section while the more secluded night zone occupies the pre-existing building.

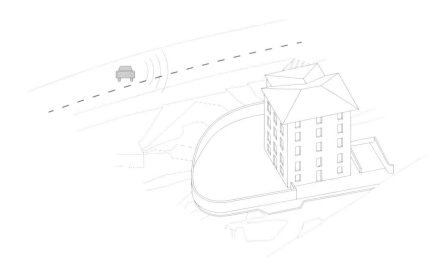

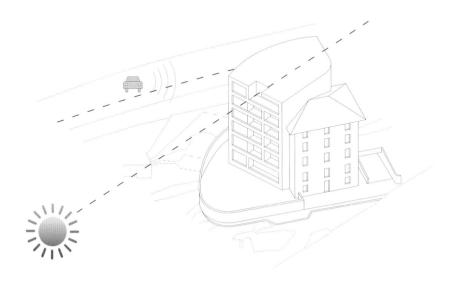

Meta-design embraces practical, material and construction aspects. **This *modus operandi* not only includes the compositional aspect of a project but also construction systems and façade materials.** In this case, the façade of the pre-existing house was plastered with the same lime plaster mix originally used. The new shell is made up of a double skin of terracotta bricks, which intermediate insulation, the outer surface coated with hand-applied lime plaster to which a protective layer comprising natural bee's wax was applied, that allows it to last over time, resisting the aggression of adverse weather conditions.

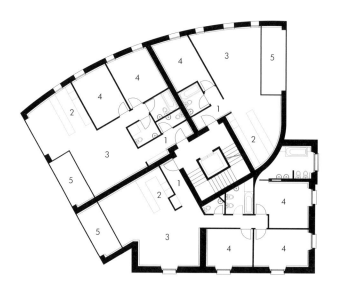

First floor plan

1. Atrium
2. Kitchen
3. Living area
4. Bedroom
5. Loggia

m   0 1 2 3 4 5 6

Although obvious and universally recognized, an architect must start from simple practical considerations, bearing in mind how strongly rooted in our unconscious is the desire for protection in shelters that are part of a harmonious community.

Each of us lives out this unconscious state in different ways. Our shelters are part of complex interconnected aggregations bound by functional and social tenets underpinned by an innate drive to constantly improve and evolve.

The architect has a great responsibility
to the community and its context.

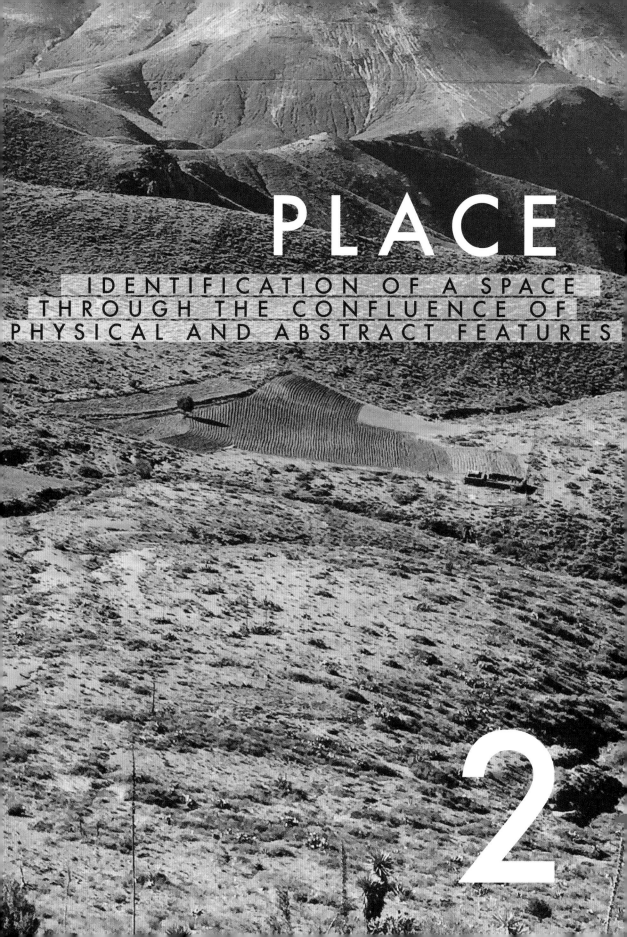

PLACE

IDENTIFICATION OF A SPACE
THROUGH THE CONFLUENCE OF
PHYSICAL AND ABSTRACT FEATURES

2

Today, more so than in the past,
architecture is a small pixel in the urban fabric.

NATURE, ARCHITECTURE, URBANIZATION

Man's relentless occupation of land has made environmental safeguard an urgent issue. All major international organizations and institutions concerned with the health of our planet appeal for a plan to mitigate the harmful effects of ever growing emissions into the atmosphere, the cause of global warming. Our studio theorizes and puts into practice ways in which architecture can reduce harmful emissions, adopting construction features conducive to re-establishing an indispensable balance between the constant expansion of urbanization and the natural world. Urban development in recent years has often led to an exponential increase in urban density with scant regard for geographical or geological features. We must now commit to safeguarding our landscape from unbridled urban sprawl. **Nature, architecture and urbanization are macro-systems rooted in the physical and abstract. Both must be recognized if we are to fully grasp what is at stake. Geopolitics, history, the economy, sociology, religions, and regulations are only some of the features that characterize the essence of a place.** Switzerland's Canton Ticino, home to generations of creative architects, is often taken as an example of a region that has preserved the environmental quality of a landscape considered among the most beautiful in Europe. The projects illustrated here – among the first developed by Mino Caggiula Architects – aim to achieve high standard residential architecture but also restore environmental livability. This has been attained with the systematic use of natural vegetation, placing structures underground, and carefully balancing built cubic meters with reconstituted natural habitat. It is a design philosophy based on the study of archetypes and development models that meet both client requirements and the demand by the collectivity that nature, architecture and urbanization dialogue in harmony. Identifying that 'logical' equilibrium to be achieved when a built structure is included in the landscape is therefore a project priority, an approach we have negotiated with all clients of our completed works and which we continue to adopt.

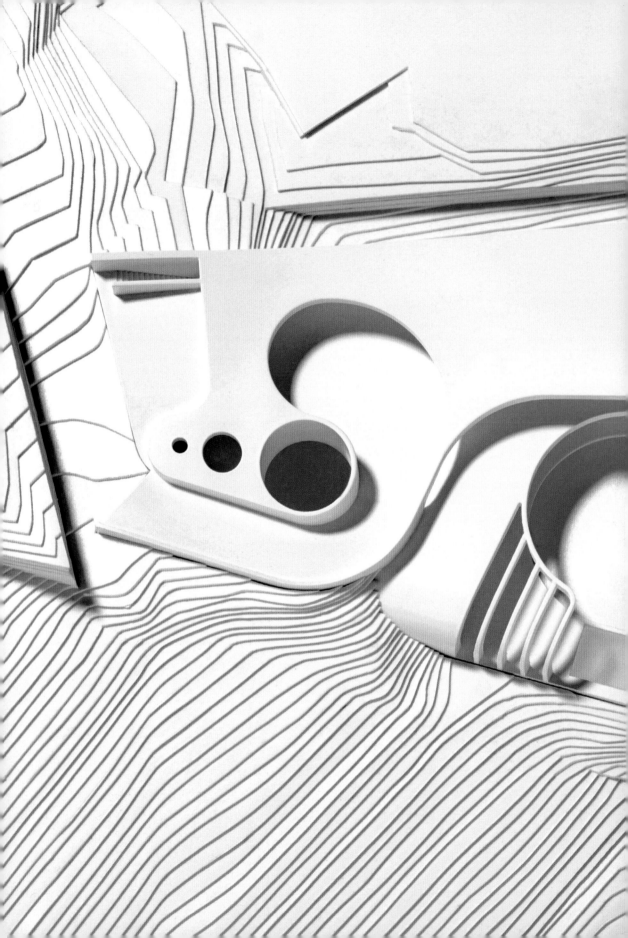

Building a model with my own hands is the most congenial way of understanding the psyche and morphology of a place.

"My new atelier is not a box but an architecture full of movement, like my sculptures."

Alice Trepp

ATELIER TREPP

Artist Alice Trepp models sculptures with her hands, immortalizing moments in time. Although architects are often called artists, real artists are those who create works of art. Artists work on their subject while architects get people to live inside what they build. From the initial inspiration through to the actual construction, innumerable relationships are developed involving the client, specialists, and craftsmen, each in their own way constrained by pre-established costs and deadlines.

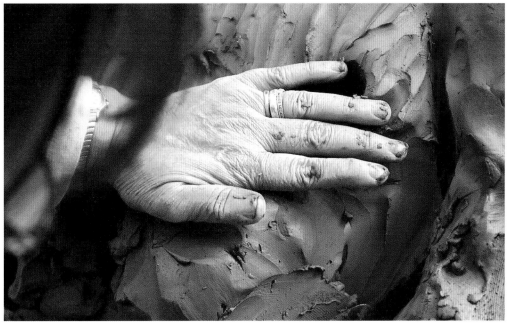

Rosa
Alice Trepp, 2016

The *Trepp Atelier* was developed for a person but also for a place. Building an artist's atelier first of all means interpreting the place in terms of that artist's work. Indeed, designing an atelier to mirror the thought and philosophy of an artist has long fascinated generations of artists and the architects charged with the task. Located near Origlio, a village overlooking the lake of the same name, Alice Trepp's studio is both a place of work and a home. Built to slot as naturally as possible into the contour lines forming the morphology of the site, the house enjoys splendid views over an unspoiled landscape against a backdrop of distant mountains. **Placed mainly underground, it takes its cue from ancient Greek theaters that were molded to fit into the natural morphology of their context. Built to be part of the landscape, the artist's atelier/home is a shelter from which to contemplate the natural world under the changing light and draw inspiration.**

The Greek theater of Stratos
IV-II Century AC, Aetolia-Acarnania, Greece

The project concept developed out of a study of the natural contours of the area. Wedged into the two highest upward-curving contour lines, the building fits seamlessly into the sinuous lie of the land. **The volume takes shape rising like leaves out of the ground to make the architecture appear a natural landscape feature. An iconic touch has been added by pivoting the construction around a 'cenote', in acknowledgement of the artist's Ecuadorian origins.** Built around this core, the two stories intersect, creating a dynamic play of transparency and visual permeability. Interior and exterior spaces blend and re-form, constantly interacting with the light and the surrounding countryside.

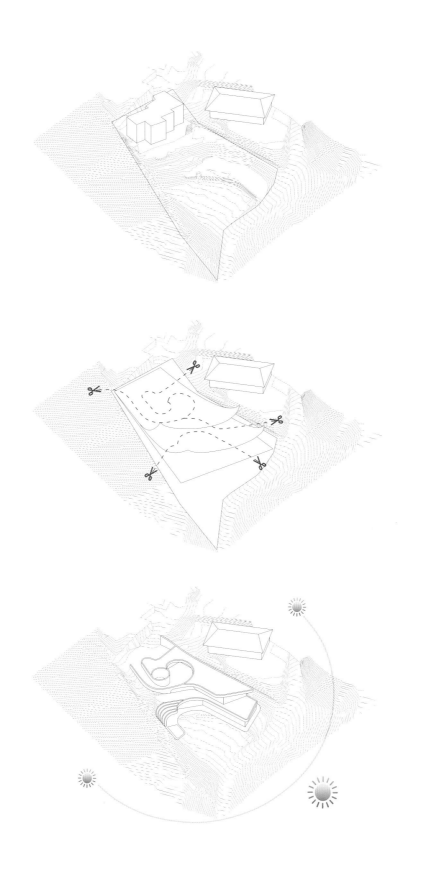

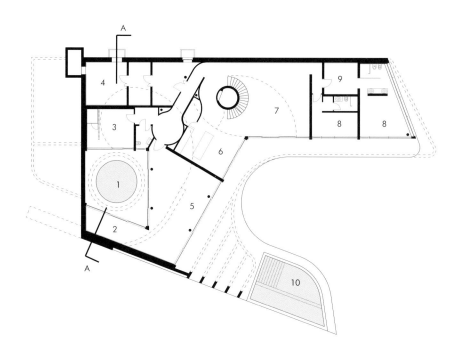

First floor plan

1. Cenote
2. Plaster room
3. Spa
4. Utility room
5. Artist's studio
6. Kitchen
7. Living room
8. Bedroom
9. Closet
10. Biopool

m   0 1 2 3 4 5 6

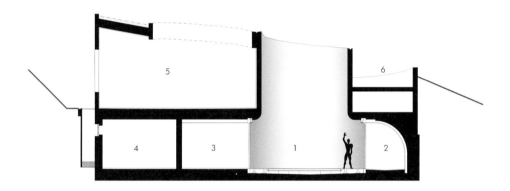

Section AA

1. Cenote
2. Plaster room
3. Spa
4. Utility room
5. Main entrance
6. Vehicle access ramp

m   0   1   2   3   4   5   6

Cenote Ik Kil,
Yucatàn, Mexico

Cenote. A naturally formed depression in the earth created by tectonic movements; a space filled with light, vegetation and water.

The cenote in *Atelier Trepp* is a space of contemplation and communion with nature. Reflected, refracted light playing on water is conducive to a multi-sensorial awareness of the passing of time. The cenote acts as a sundial as the day proceeds and the light changes, capturing the fleeting moments of the day. The freshness coming off the water, the light breeze that gently sways the sweet-smelling overhanging vegetation, the twittering of birds, and the view of the passing clouds conjure up visions of the artist lying on the gravel of the shallow water immersed in a moment of sensory exploration – the search for the sublime in the everyday, a moment of contemplation for the artist before, during and after the creation of a work of art.

MODELS, RESEARCH AND REPRESENTATION

Architecture has always used various ways of producing a realistic, plausible image of what the architect has in mind: models, meta-design ideograms, and 3D graphics diagrams. Today, digital simulation software produces hyper-realistic narrative models of what is to be. Our studio uses a broad raft of manual and digital tools, selecting the most appropriate form of representation according to the characteristics and complexity of the project in hand. All new projects begin with the building of a scale model of the contour lines of the site and its surroundings against which the proposed forms and components of the new architecture are assessed. **The scale model is an indispensable analysis, study and communication tool throughout the various development phases, a uniquely tangible object combining place, project and the individual. Scale models allow the designer to work with a series of superimposed elements following tectonic principles and construction processes.** Not only central to the practice of building, the scale model is also a strategic communication tool in relations with the client. Being able to show the series of component parts simplifies description, giving a clear idea of the spaces, load-bearing structures, spatial partitions and other features of the future building.

How we build on the land must resolve the complex interweave of natural landscapes and built-up areas.

The synergy between the nature of a place and the hand of man is the quintessence of creativity.

A new architecture or the manipulation of pre-existing elements transforms the natural setting; it is an act of alteration. The place must generate architecture, and vice-versa, in a well-balanced thoughtful way.

BLADE

A luxury residential complex, the *Blade* project tackled the question of blending a manmade construction harmoniously into the landscape while at the same time offering occupants sweeping views over Lake Lugano. Once again, the project goes beyond the question of how a building and the landscape blend to explore the relationship of the individual with the natural world. **The concept was inspired by the works of the American artist Richard Serra, whose famous metal sculptures have often become so integrated into their site as to be landmarks.** Similarly, the *Blade* project 'scratches' the hillside as a gentle re-appropriation of nature by man.

Blades of curved Cor-ten steel are positioned to overlook and leave intact the wooded area to the south and direct the complex and views towards the lake. The curvature of the 220 meter steel blade was calculated so that the sagitta of the chord of the circle described never exceeds 1 mm every linear meter. As well as making the interiors easy to furnish, this curvature follows the scale of the landscape, creating the dualism achieved by Serra's sculptures, resulting in a mimetic, partly underground architecture in keeping to comply with the slope and scale of the terrain. **The creative features underpinning the *Blade* project can be summed up in the harmony achieved between built space and the surrounding landscape, the alternation of solids and voids, the tension created between the different forms, and the inclusion of natural vegetation.** Two distinct blocks ensure lake views from every residential unit, each separated from the other by a system of primary and secondary partitions or blades that divide the interiors and create the loggias and terraced gardens, extending the indoor living areas onto the outside. Like the blade partitions, the natural vegetation spreading over the paved areas creates horizontal and vertical divisions but also connections.

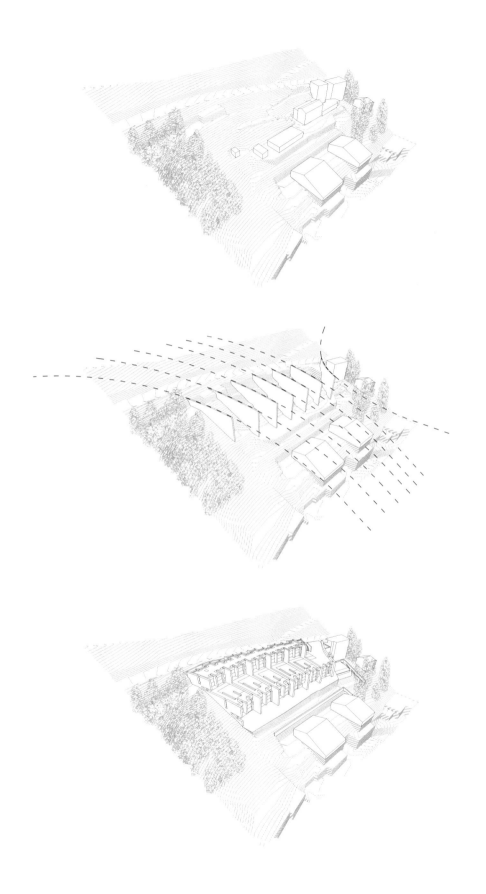

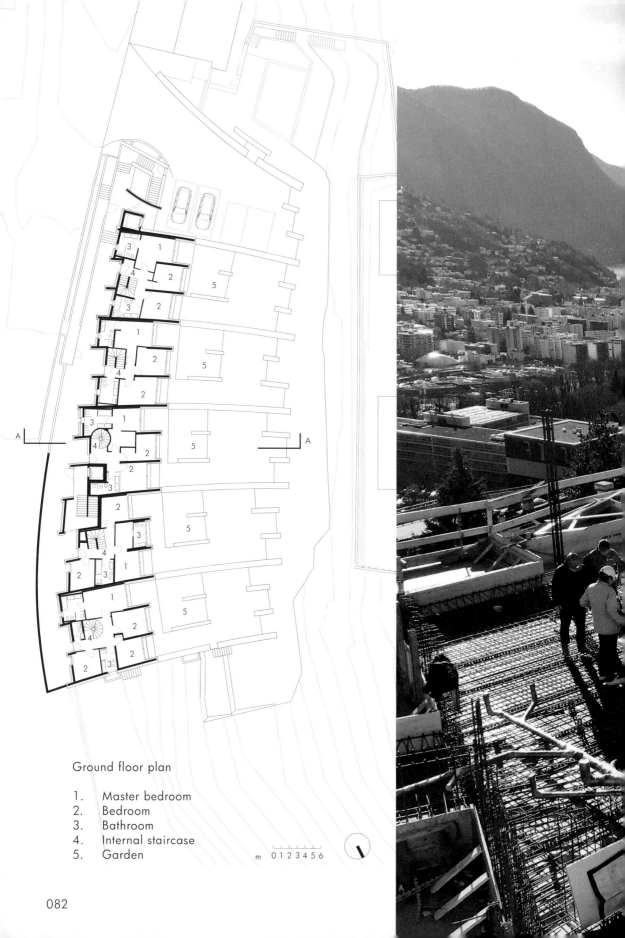

Ground floor plan

1. Master bedroom
2. Bedroom
3. Bathroom
4. Internal staircase
5. Garden

m 0 1 2 3 4 5 6

Installation "The matter of time"
Richard Serra, 1994-2005, Guggenheim Museum Bilbao, Spain

Inspiration can spring from the most unexpected places and moments. **Time and observation teach us how our actions, as well as many of our thoughts and sensations are simply a distillate of lived experiences retained as memories.** The same process gives rise to architecture: connections and deep-seated memories of things that are part of us unconsciously rise to the surface, impulses that manifest as we develop an equilibrium between elements that together create architecture.

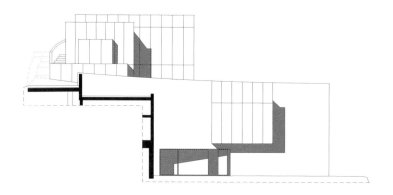

North elevation

m 0 1 2 3 4 5 6

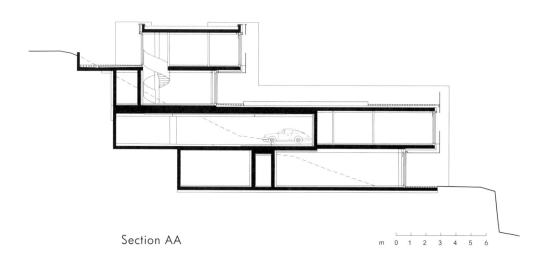

Section AA

m 0 1 2 3 4 5 6

CONCEPT

RELATING BASELINE REQUIREMENTS AND ARCHITECTURE

3

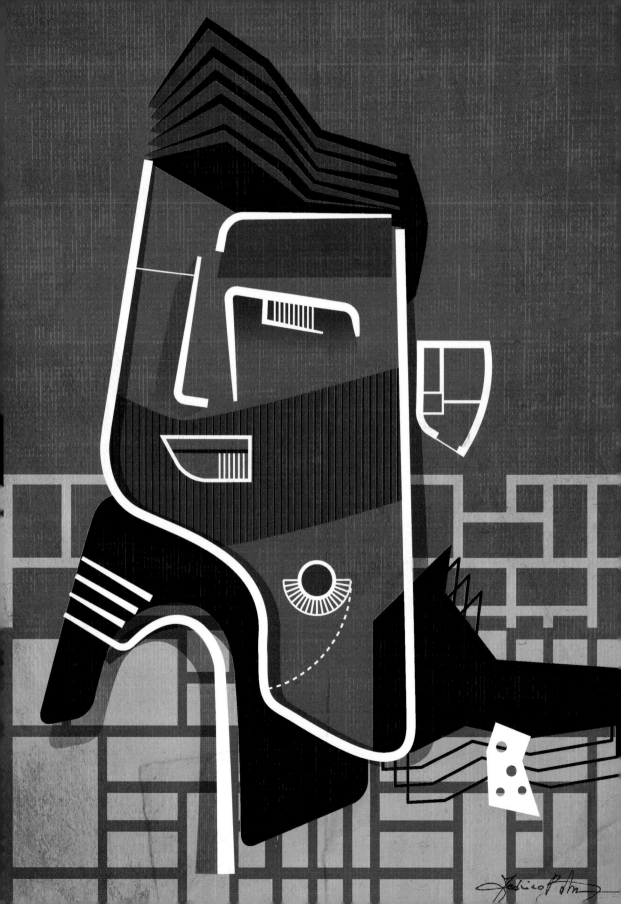

DRIVING CONCEPT

Architecture can be defined as the discipline that imparts form and structure to space by realizing a construction using technical skills and creative ability. Architectural projects must evidence how that space is conceived, its physical characteristics and how the occupant or observer interacts with it. The term 'space' is often described coupled with an adjective. We talk of imagined, virtual, represented and built space. The notion of space is open to broad interpretation, each descriptive category susceptible of becoming a conceptual possibility. **Everything starts with abstract ideas, ideogram-like images from our lived experience that then become architecture. The ultimate aim is not, however, to deliver an 'aesthetically pleasing' image but rather to embed the specific requirements revealed by the initial study into the architecture created.** Space is therefore a wide field of research whose significance goes well beyond the confines of the physical and the visual. All this is contained and metabolized in our work, a process imbued with values and alive with potential, underlining the close relationship between architecture and the arts. These motivations are in many ways articulated and metabolized in our work, in order to constantly reiterate the density of values and the potential that can arise, but also the close relationship between architecture, the arts and the multiplicity of disciplines and concepts resulting from our contemporaneity. A metaphor, able to relate from its creation to its realization, with the complexity of current topics. Keywords to be analyzed from time to time, according to the needs of people and places, simplifying and crystallizing thoughts in built architecture, with the aim of adapting flexibly to constantly changing needs.

Archiportrait Mino Caggiula
Illustration by Federico Babina

TERRITO

CONCEP

RELIGIO

FRENZY

LIVING

EVOLUTION

HERITAGE AGE SOCIA

MOTION

EC

TEAMWORK

COMMUNITY

SUSTAINABILITY

COEXISTENCE FU

SECTORISATION

FUN CARE

CULTURE

INCLUSION

ANSITION PLAYFULNESS

LOCATION

HUMAN BEING

ONISM GEOPOLITICS EN

ISM NECE

NIZZA PARADISE RESIDENCE

The *Nizza Paradise Residence* in Lugano was one of the most challenging projects built by the practice on account of the complex topography of the site. Made up of historic buildings and new constructions, Lugano's skyline is undergoing constant transformation characterized by increasing densification. The curving shape of the *Nizza Paradise Residence* resembling the sinuous silhouette of a reclining woman, instills a sense of calm as it follows the gently natural slope, at the foot of Mount St. Salvatore, a transformation of the curve line in architecture. Winner of a competition by invitation, Mino Caggiula Architects' proposal is one of the studio most significant achievements on account of its location, massing, construction complexity, visibility, and dialogue with the client.

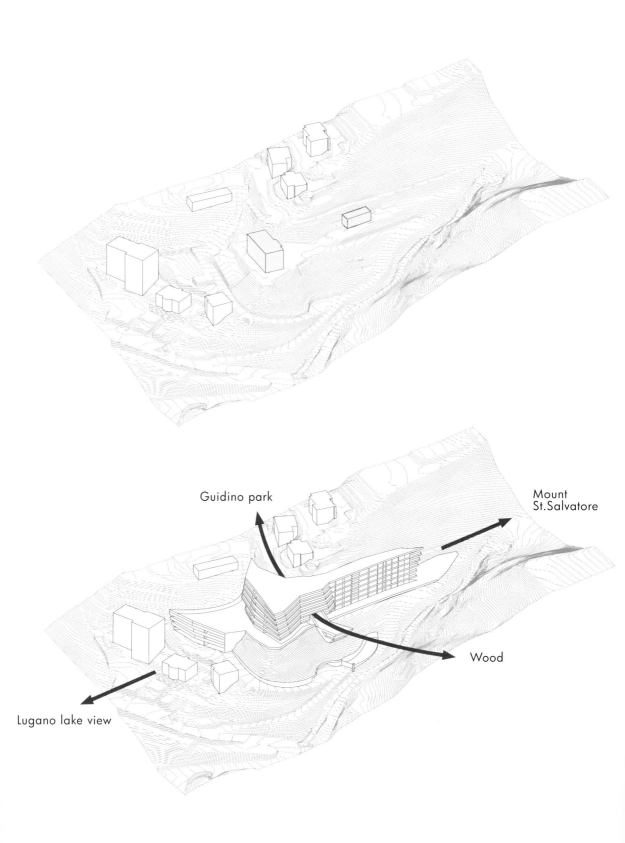

Guidino park

Mount
St.Salvatore

Wood

Lugano lake view

The architectural features that characterize the intervention, in the logic of the best possible harmonization, offer a double point of observation: from the outside, the nature and the forest of the surrounding context, from the inside the view towards Lugano, its basin and the landscape that defines the contours at the edge of the mirror of the lake. Thus a multiple dimension of perception and enjoyment, individual and collective. If analyzed from this point of view, the building reveals inside a geometric continuity that seems to accompany the profile of the landscape, in search of a sequence of signs and and backgrounds able to enhance the relationship with light, the relationship with vegetation, in search of a new possible harmony. **The site's 'macro' and 'micro' features were the basis for the subsequent architecture. The park, wood, intertwining paths, Monte San Salvatore, and the view of the lake were fundamental elements in forming the design of the volume and floor plan.** The key feature of the plan is the volume that sweeps upward, its inevitable impact on the landscape softened by a geometry that follows the curving contour lines up the slope. The façade design creates a series of different outlooks for each apartment depending on its position on the plan. The iridescent cladding blends into the landscape, giving the impression of an ineffably 'lightweight' architecture nestled into its surroundings.

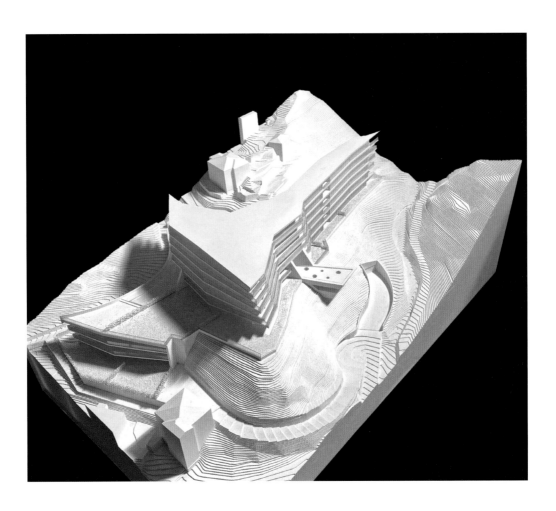

From east to west, from dawn to sunset, light penetrates into the deepest corners, slipping between the exterior and architectural features. Pedestrian pathways highlight the series of solids and voids inside the complex, flanked by a green wall facing the adjacent park, which becomes an integrated part of the overall setting. The elevation overhang clearly signposts the main entrance to the arriving visitor. The internal pathway ends as a cantilevered reflective pool reaching out towards the wood. Underneath the cantilever, a residents' spa also seems to be part of the surrounding wood. Configuration, materials, textures and colors blend the *Nizza Paradise Residence* into its surroundings from the viewpoint of the outside observer, at the same time creating an immersive visual experience for the occupants. **Refracting, reflective plays of moving light, greenery, water and metal mingle to give the residence an ever-changing aspect as the day proceeds.** Light is the matter with which to paint in architecture.

Ground floor plan

1. Outer hall
2. Reflective pool
3. Outdoor swimming pool
4. Green wall
5. Private gardens
6. Loggias

m 0 4 8 12 16 20

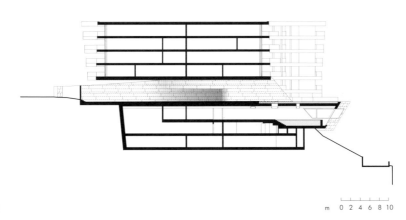

Section AA

m 0 2 4 6 8 10

The communal spaces fostering interpersonal relations, the construction itself, and the place are all specific features of this architecture. **The *Nizza Paradise* was conceived as an appendix to the Guidino park. They become a single entity with the paths that cross and mark out the boundaries of the public space. The result is an attractive inclusive area, blending public, semi-public and private space in a way that mirrors the lifestyle of both residents and park users.** The natural environment all around the complex becomes the fulcrum of a wider system in which the building takes on different functions also in terms of its perception. Today more than ever, architecture must respond to needs and circumstances that change with each brief, meeting the expectations of the individual, but also responding to collective requirements, creating attractive new areas of socialization, and transforming space into an enjoyable livable habitat.

DESIGN AND 'AESTHETIC ADDED VALUE'

Although it is true that beauty lies in the eyes of the beholder, there nonetheless is a universally shared idea of beauty. **Timeless elements and forms trigger in each of us innate, inexplicably similar sensations - biological responses that have contributed to the development of our species.** In the last decade, industrial production has radically changed. Alongside serial production there has been a proliferation of craft items. This has narrowed the distance between products coming off an automated assembly line and hand-crafted objects, marking the passage from a society based on mass production to a new reality in which values, tastes and different consumption patterns now live side by side. In architecture, the idea of value added can testify to critical sensitivity, the ability of the designer to produce a design for a given context. While respecting the existing equilibria, this new design contributes new value in terms of added form, function, and usefulness for both the individual and the community by imbuing space with a more imaginative universal value. Changing scale and going from a designed object to architecture, a building contributes to the wider urban landscape, both as an object in itself, falling within or outside recurrent aesthetic parameters, but also as a catalyst in the environment, a focal element in the life of a community.

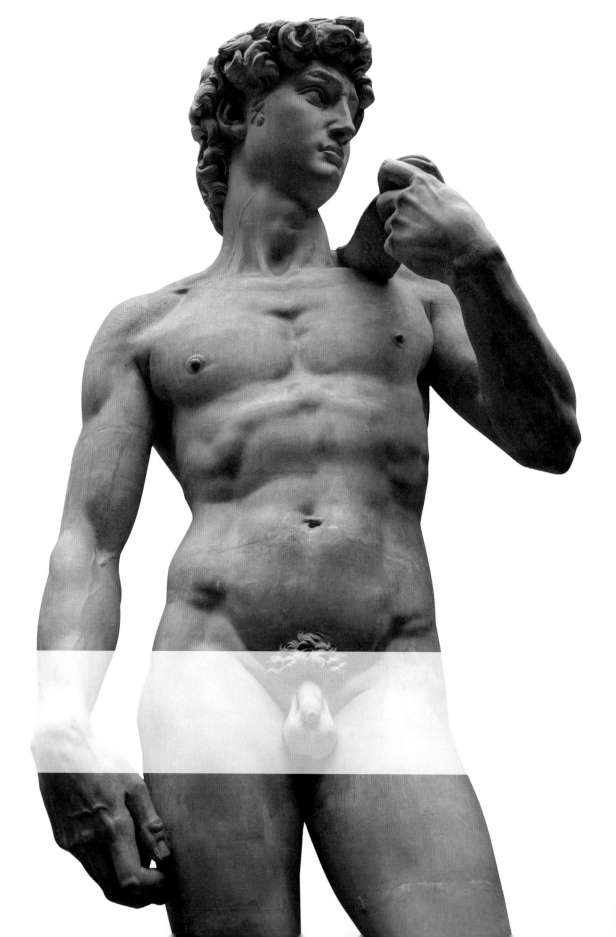

The canon of beauty is the aesthetic ideal acknowledged by society. It is closely linked to the period and the cultural, economic and social condition of people.

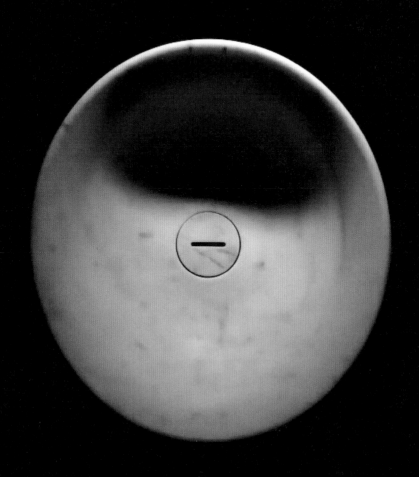

VITRUVIO

Mino Caggiula Architects partnered the famous design company, Antoniolupi, creating a free standing washbasin, given the symbolic name of *Vitruvio* as a tribute to the famous drawing by Leonardo da Vinci today in Venice's Gallerie dell'Accademia. The human figure enclosed in a square and a circle – two perfect, timeless archetypal forms, representing, say scholars, the Earth and the heavens respectively – was the initial inspiration for this designer object. The body of the washbasin is made from a single block of marble first roughed out by a digital marble cutting machine and then hand-finished by master craftsmen. **A process of 'extrusion' marries a parallelepiped and a circular section, combining two different volumes, the square 'metamorphosing' into a circle as it rises vertically from the earth to the sky.** Here too, despite the very different scale, the same design principles apply as in large-scale architecture: sleek recognizable forms that spring from an abstract concept, a memory or a recollection that lose nothing of their functional pertinence. Going from the wider urban scale to the object, meta-design is still driven by references to a specific place, in this case, the 'Pozzo di Tegna', at Ponte Brolla in Switzerland's Vallemaggia. In nature, water caresses stone, smoothing it to perfection like the expert hand of the craftsman. This was the material and sensory narrative that turned an abstract meta-design vision into a physical object.

Uomo Vitruviano,
Leonardo da Vinci, about 1490, *Gallerie dell'Accademia*, Venice

Ponte Brolla,
Vallemaggia, Ticino, Switzerland

PRÊT-À-HABITER

Prêt-à-habiter is the name of the villa built in Montagnola on the renowned Collina d'Oro hill near Lugano. **A work of particular symbolic value, the result of research into the archetypes of detached homes, a project for a user profile that is not yet known.** Commissioned by a developer for a broad market target, the program was not designed with a particular end-user in mind, as is usually the case when client and future homeowner participate in the development process. The house features all the functional symbols of residential architecture. The extensive glazing, interior staircase connecting the two stories, living area, more secluded private zones, outdoor greenery and swimming pool tick all the functional and aesthetic boxes. Here recomposed in clear-cut rigorous geometries, they become fully accessible and amenable to any future inhabitant. Closed glazed façades, interior partitions, materials and finishings create a single neutral unit suggesting possible functions for the future occupant.

Modulor in concrete at Unité d'Habitation
Marseille, France

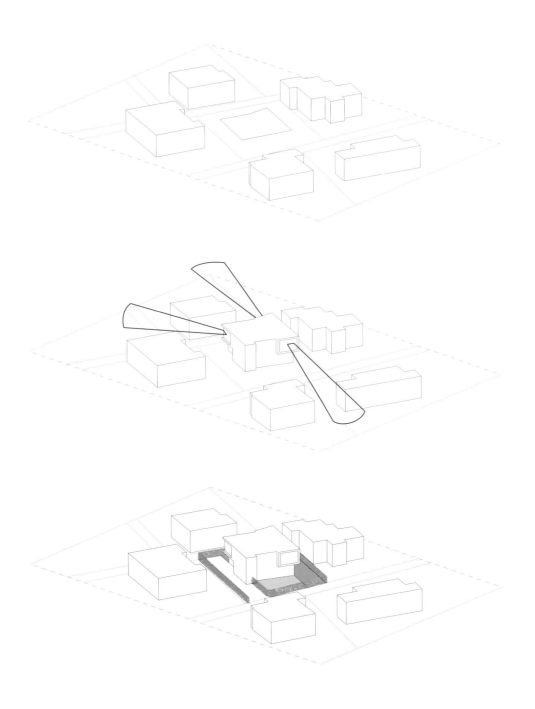

A sense of belonging comes about when people feel an integral part of the architecture around them. **It is the basis for creating architecture that responds to the human dimension. Concepts like Prêt-à-Porter, Prêt-à-Manger, and Prêt-à-Habiter reveal man's unconscious yearning to possess and consume symbols of social belonging.** Privacy becomes multi-faceted, in plan and section, made up of different heights and levels. The upper level of the external south-facing side wall is completely windowless to shield occupants from prying eyes. At the same time, it serves as a wall beam allowing a column-free ground floor. This in turn affords visual permeability through the large sliding glazed surface, continuing the private interior living space into the wider community. The sightlines between the pre-existing buildings orientate both outside observers and occupants inside the house. The archetypes of any architecture are thus measured in relation to the anthropized and naturalistic features of the place. Fair-face concrete, natural greenery and lake are all here reinterpreted. The lake is sublimated in the deck-level pool whose proximity to the house seems to be inviting the natural landscape inside. Indoors, architecture and landscape play off one another from different perspectives at different points. Light is reflected and refracted off the rough outer skin and the exterior and interior double-height surfaces.

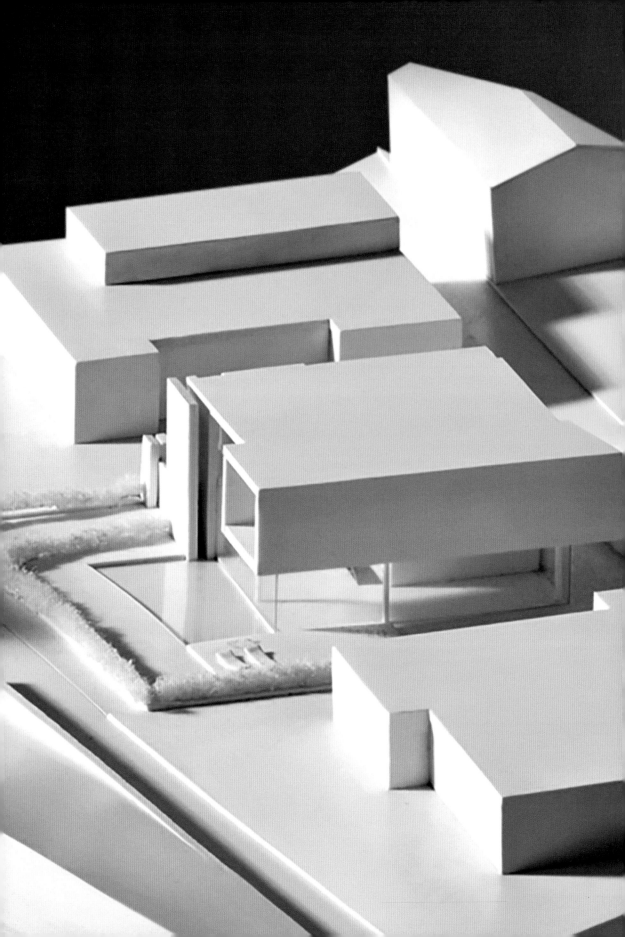

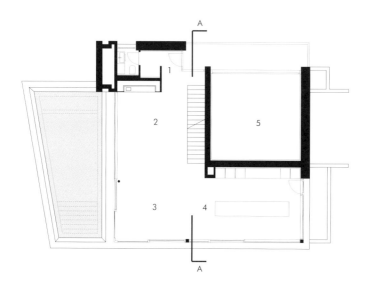

Ground floor plan

1. Atrium
2. Living area
3. Dining area
4. Kitchen
5. Garage

0 1 2 3 4 5 6

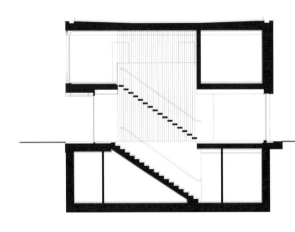

Section AA   m 0 1 2 3 4 5 6

WELL-BEING

HUMAN BEINGS AND THE ENVIRONMENT: THE IDEAL EQUILIBRIUM

+1

ERGONOMICS AND ARCHITECTURE

Le Corbusier insisted that architectural projects be preceded by careful ergonomic research. His studies, especially his *Modulor*, show what he meant by anthropometric investigation related to architecture. While our own approach begins with this analysis, we take a new perspective on these theories, including psychological and emotional aspects of the human condition. **The aim is to develop projects that not only integrate with the physical and manmade context but also fit with our behavioral patterns and psychophysical well-being.** Even if shared by us all, human reactions vary from one individual to another. Studying the ergonomics of a place also means investigating alternative or utopian models to create architecture in line with human needs. The architect today finds himself having to pull together multiple interdisciplinary aspects. This 'analog' approach has, however, probably had its day on account of the complexity introduced by the new frontiers of technology and sustainability. We must seize the opportunities offered by the widespread use of information technology and data management systems based on forecasting algorithms. Indeed, this is probably the direction architecture will be made to take in the future, since it is part of an economic system increasingly impacted by the gradual introduction of artificial intelligence systems. A scenario is taking shape in which architecture will be conceived as a vector of development, allowing an increasingly symbiotic relationship between the individual and the environment, living and working space, in other words, a new sort of ergonomics in architecture.

Design Museum Project
Mino Caggiula Architects, 2006, Parco Sempione, Milano, Italy

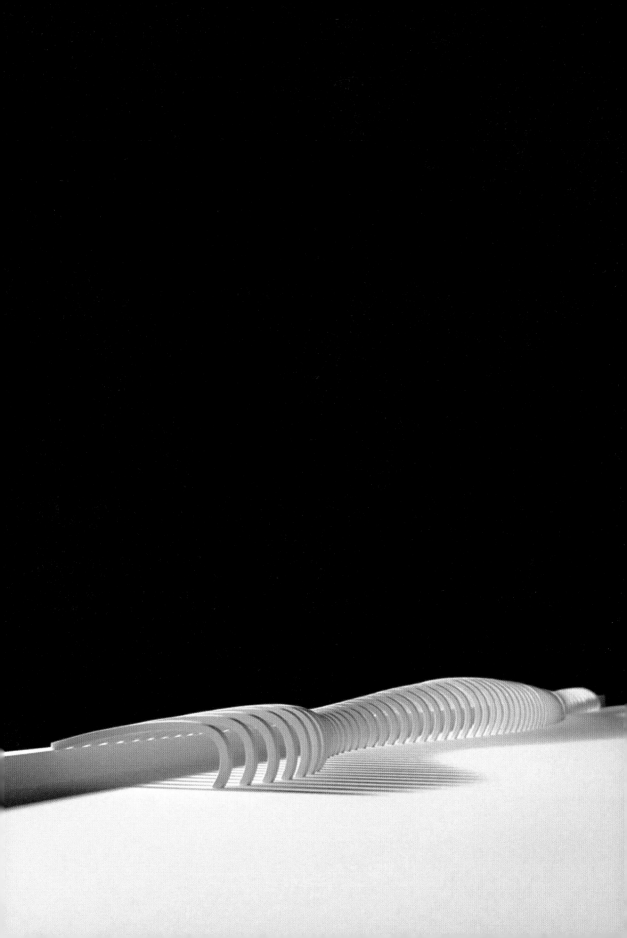

Once it becomes an actual building, architecture is made of light, matter, and memory. Our lived experience in a given place forges indelible memories. The most intimate sensations of body and mind bring back to us an instant just lived or still to come. Architecture is appreciated and every detail 'savored' through sight, hearing, smell and touch. It is up to the architect to find a healthy sensory balance, the key to a better symbiotic exchange between man, the environment and architecture. Architecture embraces both the subjective and collective spheres, the reactions triggered between individuals in that dense 'liquid' pool of fluctuating sensations. In this sense, architecture becomes a space of representation, life's stage, the real yet metaphorical backdrop of contemporary existence.

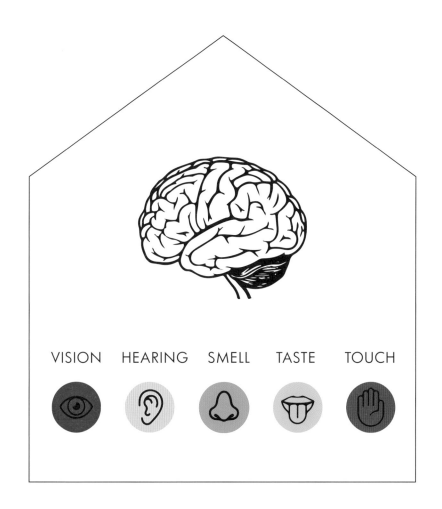

VISION   HEARING   SMELL   TASTE   TOUCH

"The Endless Liquidity of people", LIQUIDITY #4
Ian Ghent, 2018, New York City, USA

OFFICINE X

The research carried out by our practice in recent years has led us to think deeply about the relationship between man and architecture; how to create an optimal rapport between humans and their natural or built environment and do so in such a way as to safeguard an essential balance yet look to future developments with critical, aspirational proposals. This project aims to take into account the changes that are taking place and that will come, anticipating as much as possible the future needs and even the questions that inevitably the world of architecture will have to ask itself, to think about a better future. *Officine X* is an architecture to be developed in the United Arab Emirates, in a specific site of intervention, with the client's aim to settle in the most 'fertile' place today, respecting the plurality of themes and options related to the future of humanity (*Expo 2021 Connecting Minds, Creating the Future*).

The brief entails creating a first Hub 1.0 where research centers in the five continents are all interconnected, forming a true community working together on sustainability, climate change, and lifestyles, united in the pursuit of well-being. The architecture can be described as the center's 'hardware' while the activities and practices having to do with the occupants' psychophysical and environmental well-being are the 'software', that will be constantly updated and optimized. The way we translate these values into a real-life project always includes the physical and rational dimension, i.e. features like site morphology and climate conditions, but also the psychological, irrational aspects of the place: its social organization, the place of the individual, the economic and historical context. It follows that the terms **Environment**, **Motion**, **Nutrition** and **Cognition** are key concepts in our theoretical reflections, fundamental to our objective of making these values universally accessible.

SUSTAINABILITY
CLIMATE CHANGE
LIFESTYLE
MAIN ARCHITECTURAL ITEMS

ART

ARTIST RESIDENCIES
EXHIBITIONS
WORKSHOPS
MATERIAL LABS
PERFORMING ARTS
INSTALLATIONS

TECHNOLOGY

3D MODELLING
3D PRINTING
SW PROGRAMMING
VR SYSTEMS
ROBOTICS
ARTIFICIAL INTELLIGENCE

DESIGN

ARCHITECTURE
DESIGN PROCESSES
DESIGN WORKSHOPS
MARKETING
STRATEGIC DESIGN
COMMUNICATION

SCIENCE

HOLISTIC SCIENCES
NATURE
ENVIRONMENTAL SCIENCES
BIOLOGY
ECOLOGY
BIO-TECHNOLOGY
HMI

EDUCATION

MULTIPLE DISCIPLINES
INTERCULTURALISM
INTEGRATION
HUMAN SCIENCES
RESEARCH

EVENTS

EXHIBITION-EVENTS
SOCIAL MEDIA EVENTS
TALKS AND CONFERENCES
FAIRS
MEDIA COMMUNICATION

FEEDING

NUTRITION
BIO-AGRICOLTURE
SENSORY ANALYSIS
FOOD CULTURE
URBAN FARMING

HOSPITALITY

RESIDENCES
SOCIAL HOUSING
SPORTS AND LEISURE
WELLNESS

OFFICINE X

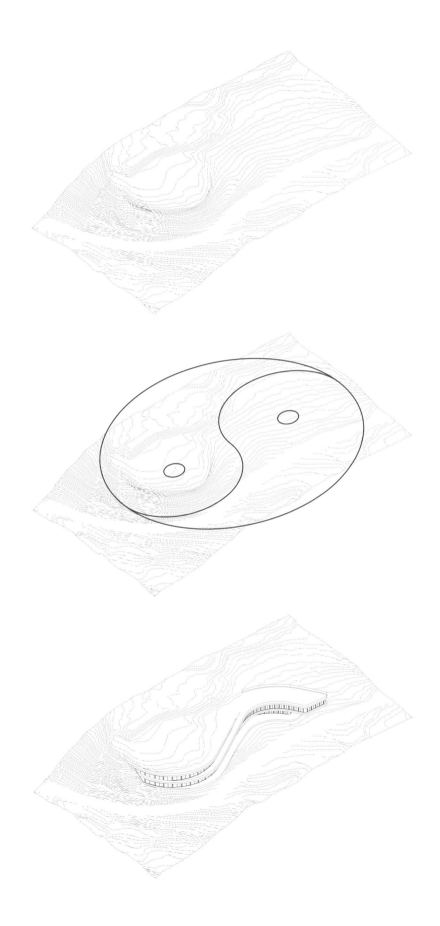

Environment. Like our habitat, our environment is both a space as well as the many relationships that make up its features and compatibility. It implies the considered use of the gray energy embedded in the materials we use, but also an awareness of the need for safeguard measures against the harmful emissions created by the act of building but also the subsequent use of our architecture.

Motion. This is our natural propensity not to stay in one place; our essential need for knowledge and development, our individual drive to create real and virtual interconnections. Here the aim is to promote sustainable mobility in terms of beneficial physical activity.

Nutrition. Underpinning the theme of growth and expansion is the whole question of 'Feeding the planet', to take up one of the claims of the most recent international exhibitions (*Expo Milan 2015*). It means taking on board technologies and processes fundamental to providing enough food. It also means recognizing the inevitable need to change our dietary habits if we are to guarantee acceptable standards of well-being for all of humankind. Biotechnologies, innovative crop optimization systems - from private allotments to hydroponic crops - all encourage a different relationship with food and eating, encouraging the involvement of younger generations, and thus helping the safeguard of farming practices accumulated down the ages.

Cognition. An all-embracing term summing up our knowledge and awareness as individuals but also as human beings. Cognition is our ability to understand phenomena and the reasons behind them, the criticalities and positive aspects of issues, and how technology, artificial intelligence, robotics and smart homes can be harnessed to allow ever more complex ethical and political management of information and data in sync with our behavioral patterns. *Officine X* aims to study the integration of systems so as to connect all types of plant and equipment with each other, while avoiding the proliferation of the electromagnetic interference produced by Wi-Fi, Bluetooth and other radio frequency-based devices. It is a utopia that is not too far down the road. We will be able to study and profile the habits, states of mind, and psychological and physical well-being of a building's residents. Essential sensory parameters measuring light, air quality, temperature, but also providing practical suggestions on healthy eating and physical activity can be made available through a real-time operational system tailored to specific needs.

Officine X aims is to be a model, a sort of 'open source' architecture project similar to the free software platforms, where designers and experts can access jointly acquired skills and so contribute to the furthering of the project. Hence the idea of a structure or architectural plan that is as independent as possible yet adaptable to the differing climate and environmental contexts - from harsh, arid desert climes to alpine or arctic conditions. Although linked to International trade routes, the sites in question will be outside urban centers to enable the creation of reserved areas conducive to thought. The facility itself will have the dual function of research and hospitality center. Its interdependent bipolar nature will be reflected symbolically in the structure and embody the age old principles of Ying and Yang. Although rooted in a philosophical concept, the program is also pragmatic and feasible. In this sense *Officine X* is a project driving the evolution of Mino Caggiula Architects, a truly **Open Being** project that sets aside all rhetoric to help usher in real, consistent and practicable sustainability. **As a practice, our mission is not just to meet our clients expectations but to extend our conceptual horizons, something precluded by our complex and frenetic contemporary lives, which – in architecture as in other fields - has led to an uncoupling of the ideation phase and the concrete realization and use of that initial idea. Indeed our own dialogue partner, client and user will, as time proceeds, come to the realization that their needs have changed. We must be ready to anticipate this.**

BACK TO
THE FUTURE

We have decided to stop a while on our journey to collect our thoughts and look back over our past, present and 'future' experience – get our house back in order. Man has built for millennia. We have to try and assimilate the lessons of our predecessors, looking back over history, traditions, and the distinctive culture of a place and the society that has grown up in it, bearing in mind the particular moment in history of our own intervention. This is how we can respect and be accountable to future generations.

Anthropization spans through the history of mankind with countless architectures, building systems, styles and trends according to human needs. Globalization follows on expansionist logic that is hard to reconcile with sustainability, which is so praised today. In the collective imagination, sustainability is only about green issues. But ecology devoid of economic and social factors without being able to exploit present and future potential in order to meet man's actual needs and aspirations, would in fact be unsustainable.

The only untouched primordial natural environment today offering a truly pristine habitat is to be found at high altitudes, increasingly rare and inaccessible places, evidently unable to accommodate sprawling communities. Our planet is being irreversibly devastated by massive pollution and the uncontrolled unstoppable and unregulated urban sprawl of large and small constructions – built often without proper design or heedless of regulations.

We are unable to manage these macro-systems. But as we cannot turn back the clock, we architects have to do something 'big' in our small way. It is an oxymoron we must live with. Energy certifications have proliferated worldwide to create healthier architecture for man and the planet. Although not compulsory, these certifications are widely encouraged, they often collide with the client's requirements, more for economic then ethical reasons. In any event, new generation buildings increasingly belong to the western-style typology of ever more shielded constructions filtering everything that comes from outside. Looking into the future, probably our shelters will be more like 'architectural spaceships'. Perhaps one day they will even have very little to do with their context since the seemingly unstoppable destruction of our planet will wipe out all healthy places in which to build. So a journey into the past in order to go back to the future and analyze what we have learnt in the present. **Today and in the future, and as it always has been, it is the immensely valuable 'Obvious' that will allow us to go back to ways of interpreting and researching logical, practical and innovative solutions to increasingly complex problems and demands.**

This approach should be able to meet and integrate expectations in terms of both landscape and man's social needs. The aim is to be able to meet the requests of public and private clients, who today as in the past, are and will be our greatest opportunity, allowing us to constantly improve how we build on our planet, at least until this is still possible. It means taking a hard look at ourselves and being able to tackle a problem from many points of view, never thinking you have achieved the ultimate. For the present moment will already be time past in a minute.

Anamnesis, in order to develop concepts and architectures able to enhance the well-being of the planet and the individual – man's ultimate aim – the architect must first acquire a deep understanding of human needs in a given context and the most appropriate architecture to meet those needs. Conceptual and architectural aspects must go hand-in-hand with a competent technical skill set and the correct use and assembly of materials. Maximizing the benefits of this equilibrium, and taking a hard look at how this is achieved means taking on the whole sphere of technology and physical matter. Skilled craftsmen, and building methods honed over the centuries have always been at the root of civilizations as they developed over time. From the Tigris to the Euphrates in Mesopotamia through to the medieval guilds of free masons right up to our day, man has acquired, safeguarded and refined building skills, ensuring the continuity of his civilization. Today those unwritten secrets no longer exist. Today we live in a globalized economic system that incentivizes sharing of increasingly efficient innovative tools and materials, made available by the academic world and the media. Experimentation is ongoing on robots with 3-D printing capability on the scale of a building, opening up the possibility that this may one day be what the construction sector will look like. However, I believe one thing will never change: the human relationship created during the initial design and subsequent building process in which a meeting of minds and hands create constant dialogue and exchange.

Our collective intelligence is able to create projects not just for the architects and clients involved. Architecture belongs to all those who participate in creating it, living it and changing it over time. This is what leads to the empathy and timeless magic of creating architecture that needs no words to be understood. The deep instinctive emotion aroused by seeing a building gradually take shape until it stands free from the protective scaffolding and craftworkers that had shielded it for months, even years, is something that will remain with us for decades and indeed centuries to come.

Nizza Paradise worksite
Mino Caggiula Architects, 2015, Lugano, Switzerland

ACKNOWLEDGMENTS

I am grateful for my 'reversed' career path, from practice to theory, from bricklayer to architect. I am grateful for my passion, my confidence but still more for my weaknesses and doubts, and for those who stand by me, without whom this monograph would not have been possible.

I thank my family, Ylenia, Adrielle and Laís who have always supported and sustained me.

Massimo Pedrazzini, a great friend, who hosted me in New York City where I had the honor of meeting Kenneth Frampton who helped me refine my critical eye.
He introduced me to Steven Holl, the architect, who more than any other has inspired me;

I am grateful for my work experience, which has allowed me to participate in and win several international competitions,

To Elia Zenghelis, maestro and mentor, who made me think about the wider regional scale of the city before picking up a pencil.

To Michele Barra and Francesco Salinetti, who respectively gave me my first worksite experience and then allowed me to take my first steps as an architect.

I acknowledge all my clients, past present and future,

My whole team, Enrico Leonardo Fagone, and THE PLAN for making this first monograph possible.

My sincerest thanks to you all ☺

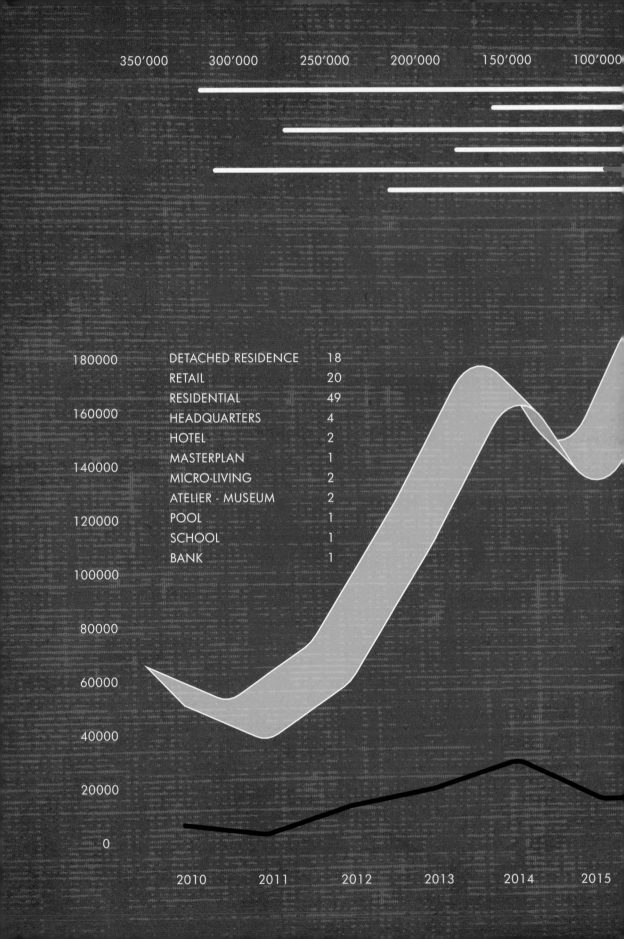

350'000   300'000   250'000   200'000   150'000   100'000

DETACHED RESIDENCE	18
RETAIL	20
RESIDENTIAL	49
HEADQUARTERS	4
HOTEL	2
MASTERPLAN	1
MICRO-LIVING	2
ATELIER - MUSEUM	2
POOL	1
SCHOOL	1
BANK	1

180000
160000
140000
120000
100000
80000
60000
40000
20000
0

2010   2011   2012   2013   2014   2015

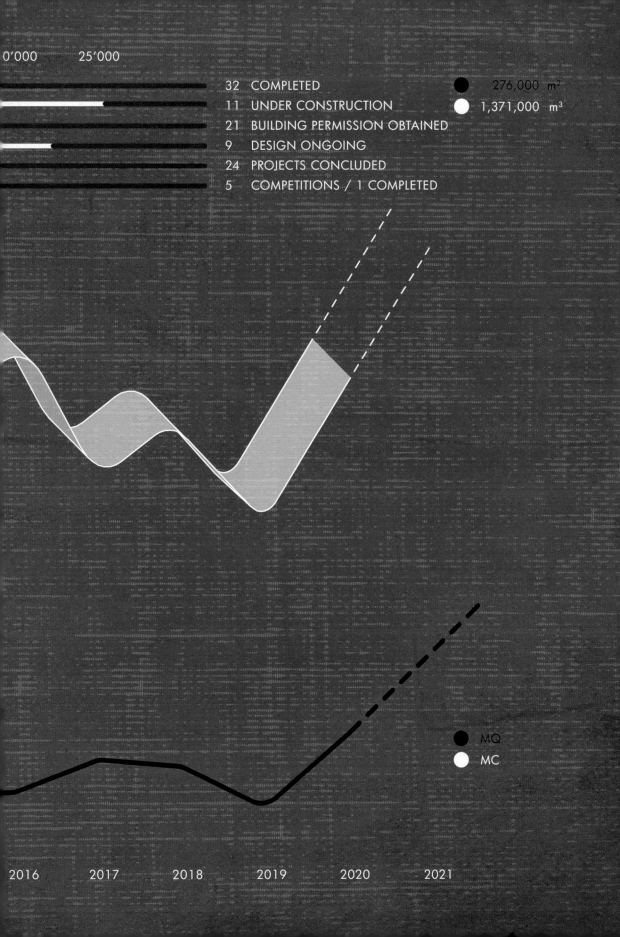

0'000   25'000

32 COMPLETED   ● 276,000 m²
11 UNDER CONSTRUCTION   ○ 1,371,000 m³
21 BUILDING PERMISSION OBTAINED
9   DESIGN ONGOING
24 PROJECTS CONCLUDED
5   COMPETITIONS / 1 COMPLETED

● MQ
○ MC

2016   2017   2018   2019   2020   2021

SUMMARY OF WORKS

1	Hotel Villa Adriana	designed	Rome, Italy	2005
2	Design Museum	designed	Milan, Italy	2006
3	Bironico Center	licenced	Bironico, Switzerland	2010
4	Viper Center	under construction	Arbedo Castione, Switzerland	2010
5	Ambrofood Center	designed	Rivera, Switzerland	2010
6	Dehor	designed	Porza, Switzerland	2010
7	Swimming Pool Villa Vito	built	Gordola, Switzerland	2010
8	Villa Lianza	built	Cugnasco, Switzerland	2010 - 2012
9	Brico Center	built	Biasca, Switzerland	2010 - 2013
10	Natuzzi Showroom	built	Zurich, Switzerland	2010
11	Paguro Residence	built	Lugano, Switzerland	2010 - 2014
12	Pojana Residence	designed	Riva San Vitale, Switzerland	2011
13	Spider Center	licenced	Massagno, Switzerland	2011
14	5 Stelle Showroom	built	Mezzovico, Switzerland	2011 - 2012
15	Bellavista Residence	designed	Gordola, Switzerland	2011 - 2012
16	Box Residence	built	Osogna, Switzerland	2011 - 2013
17	Trilogy Center	licenced	Locarno, Switzerland	2011
18	San Bernardino Residence	licenced	San Bernardino, Switzerland	2012
19	Orsenigo Residence	designed	Como, Italy	2012
20	Phuket Residence	designed	Phuket, Thailand	2012
21	Triangolo 2 Center	designed	Locarno, Switzerland	2012
22	Villa Calice	designed	Giubiasco, Switzerland	2012
23	Socar Gas Station	built	Pambio - Noranco, Switzerland	2012 - 2013
24	Take Away Restaurant	built	Bioggio, Switzerland	2012
25	Rubik Residence	built	Stabio, Switzerland	2012 - 2014
26	Villa Baldesberger	built	Curio, Switzerland	2012 - 2014
27	Triangolo 1 Center	built	Locarno, Switzerland	2012 - 2014
28	Villa Prêt-à-Habiter 1	built	Lugano-Montagnola, Switzerland	2012 - 2015
29	Villa Prêt-à-Habiter 2	built	Lugano-Brè, Switzerland	2012 - 2015
30	Villa C'Est Elle	licenced	Pura, Switzerland	2013
31	Como Calcio Sport Center	designed	Como, Italy	2013
32	Moncucco Residence	designed	Lugano, Switzerland	2013
33	Monte Cucco Residence	licenced	Gordola, Switzerland	2013
34	Villa Elisa	designed	Lugano, Switzerland	2013

35	Fortuna Residence	built	Minusio, Switzerland	2013 - 2016
36	L.E.C.H.E Park Residence	built	Bellinzona, Switzerland	2013 - 2017
37	Wry Residence	under construction	Canobbio, Switzerland	2013 - 2021
38	Hotel San Bernardino	licenced	San Bernardino, Switzerland	2014
39	Mugnee Residence	licenced	Barbengo, Switzerland	2014
40	Paciarè Residence	licenced	Arbedo, Switzerland	2014
41	Gnosca Residence	designed	Bellinzona, Switzerland	2014
42	Garage Autonec SA	licenced	Lavertezzo, Switzerland	2014 - 2015
43	Via Varenna Residence	designed	Locarno, Switzerland	2014
44	San Quirico Residence	built	Minusio, Switzerland	2014 - 2016
45	La Rotonda Residence	built	Arbedo - Castione, Switzerland	2014 - 2017
46	Nizza Paradise Residence	competititon - built	Lugano-Paradiso, Switzerland	2014 - 2017
47	Eolica Residence	built	Pregassona, Switzerland	2014 - 2018
48	Slope Center	licenced	Barbengo, Switzerland	2015
49	Montarina Residence	licenced	Montarina, Switzerland	2015
50	Villa Origlio	licenced	Origlio, Switzerland	2015
51	Icon Residence	licenced	Melide, Switzerland	2015
52	Villa Rustica	built	Lugano-Castagnola, Switzerland	2015 - 2016
53	Waves Residence	built	Savosa, Switzerland	2015 - 2017
54	Valle Maggia Center	under construction	Locarno, Switzerland	2015 - 2021
55	Lotus Residence	designed	Bellinzona, Switzerland	2016
56	Barbengo Residence	licenced	Barbengo, Switzerland	2016
57	Massagno Residence	designed	Massagno, Switzerland	2016
58	Zermatt School	competition	Zermatt, Switzerland	2016
59	Showroom Antonio Lupi	designed	Milan, Itlay	2016
60	Gentilino Residence	built	Collina d'Oro, Switzerland	2016 - 2018
61	WM System Building	built	Opatija, Croatia	2016 - 2018
62	Clouds Residence	built	Biasca, Switzerland	2016 - 2019
63	Gate Capo S. Martino	built	Paradiso, Switzerland	2016 - 2019
64	Atelier - Villa Trepp	built	Origlio, Switzerland	2016 - 2020
65	Libellula Residence	under construction	Muzzano, Switzerland	2016 - 2020
66	Blade Residence	under construction	Canobbio, Switzerland	2016 - 2020
67	Reiffeisen Bank	competition	Savosa, Switzerland	2017
68	Villa Bonalumi	licenced	Brione, Switzerland	2017

69	Dischma Residence	licenced	Lugano-Paradiso, Switzerland	2017
70	51st street Residence	designed	New York City, USA	2017
71	Garage Mezzovico	built	Mezzovico, Switzerland	2017 - 2018
72	Snake Residence	licenced	Bellinzona, Switzerland	2017
73	Noranco Residence	under construction	Noranco, Switzerland	2017 - 2020
74	Onyx Residence	built	Mendrisio, Switzerland	2017 - 2020
75	Villa ai Ronchi 1	under construction	Comano, Switzerland	2017 - 2021
76	Masterplan Bellinzago	in progress	Milan, Italy	2017
77	Swimming Pool Center	competition	Frauenfeld, Switzerland	2018
78	Ponte Capriasca Residence	under construction	Ponte Capriasca, Switzerland	2018 - 2022
79	Mirador Residence	under construction	Lugano, Switzerland	2018 - 2023
80	Wull Tower Center	designed	Pambio, Switzerland	2018
81	Bellinzona 1 Center	designed	Bellinzona, Switzerland	2018
82	Ruggia Residence	designed	Lugano, Switzerland	2018
83	Bristol Residence	built	Lugano, Switzerland	2018 - 2019
84	Villa Fartushniyak	built	Sorengo, Switzerland	2018 - 2019
85	Warsawska Student	designed	Olsztyn, Poland	2018
86	Bellinzona 2 Center	in progress	Bellinzona, Switzerland	2019
87	Miravalle Residence	under construction	Massagno, Switzerland	2019
88	Villa ai Ronchi 2	licenced	Comano, Switzerland	2019
89	Villa Mirador	licenced	Lugano, Switzerland	2019
90	Sankt Moritz Residence 1	licenced	Sankt Moritz, Switzerland	2019
91	Villa Moscia	built	Ascona, Switzerland	2019 - 2020
92	Officine X	in progress	United Arab Emirates	2020
93	Cascina Merlata Tower	competition	Milan, Italy	2020
94	Villa Castagnola	in progress	Lugano, Switzerland	2020
95	Paradiso Ghielmi	in progress	Lugano-Paradiso, Switzerland	2020
96	Breganzona Residence	under construction	Breganzona, Switzerland	2020
97	Sorengo Residence	in progress	Lugano, Switzerland	2020
98	Sankt Moritz Residence 2	in progress	Sankt Moritz, Switzerland	2020
99	Cassarate Residence	in progress	Lugano, Switzerland	2020
100	Agno Residence	in progress	Agno, Switzerland	2020
101	Lugano Sonvico Residence	designed	Lugano, Switzerland	2020

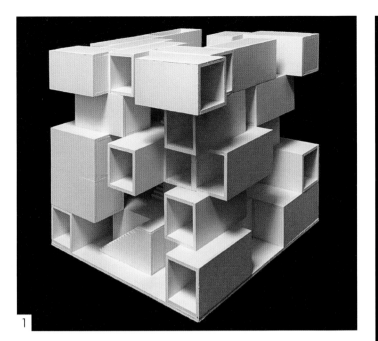

1

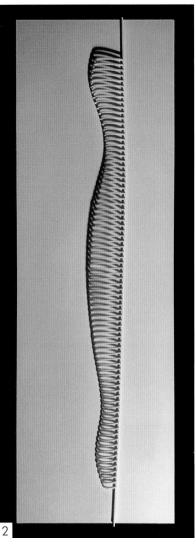

2

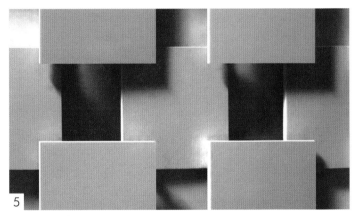

5

11

13

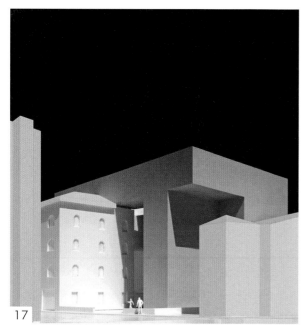

17

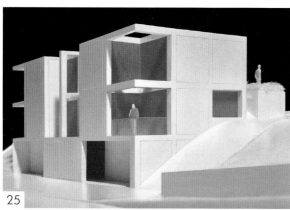

25

22

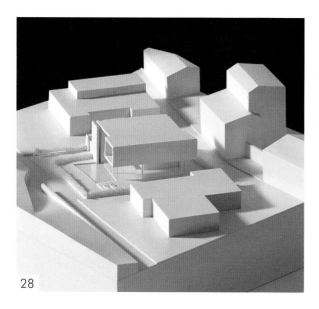

28

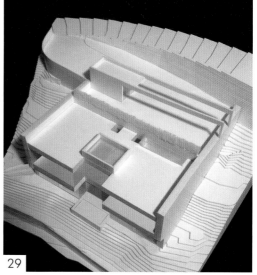

29

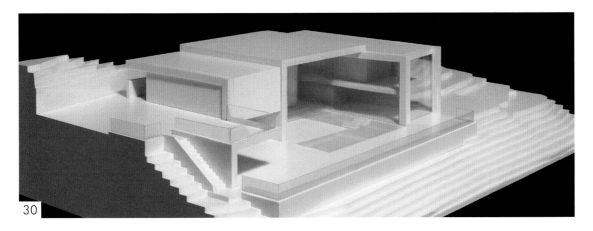

30

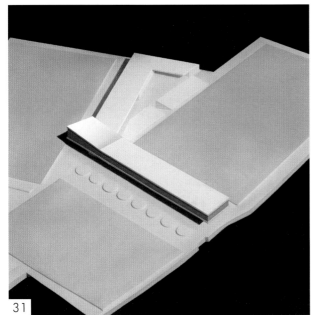

31

32

36

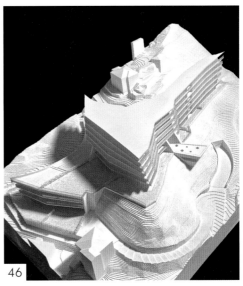

46

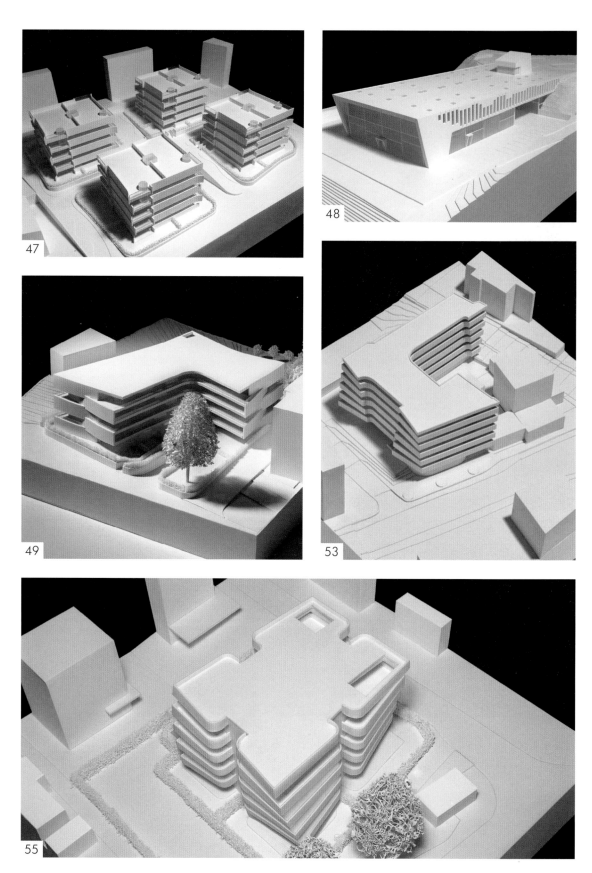

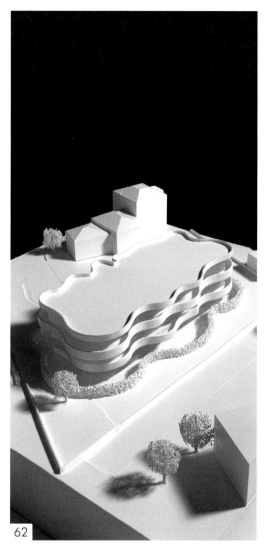

62

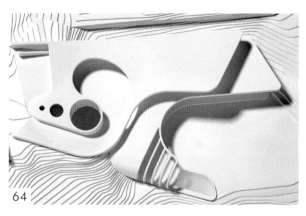

64

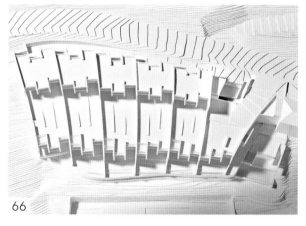

66

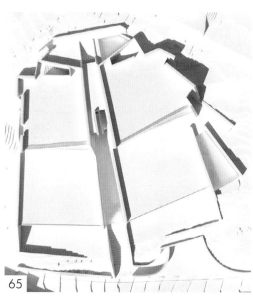

65

67

77

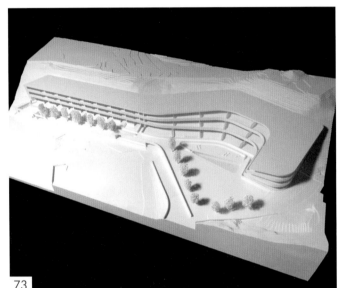

73

79

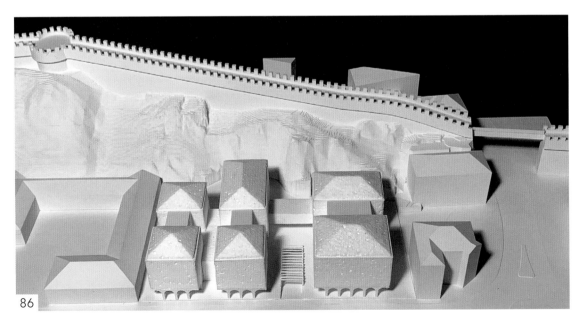

86

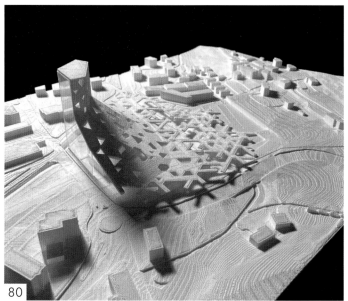

80

87

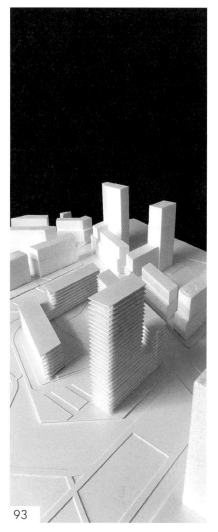

93

94

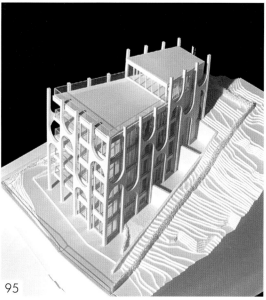

95

TEAM

Mino Caggiula Architects

PIERLUCA CARUBIA
LOREDANA CURATOLO
ANDREA MALDARIZZI
DIEGO COMPAGNO
THOMAS GIULIANI
ALBERTO CUNEO
FABIO FIORE
LUCA ZINGARO
DAVIDE CARONE
FORTESA SOFTA
JOSEPH COPES
JACOPO BIANCHINO

Freelance Collaborators

WALTER GHIONI
GIADA GHIONI
GIACOMO BRONZINI
BRUNO BRONZINI

Interns

CHRISTIAN RIZZO
RENE MARIJANOVIĆ
LINA CRIVELLI

Communication Lab

SANTI&SANTI

Visualisations

BAUMATTE

Business Development

BUSINESS UP

Former Team

FRANCESCO MAGNI
ELISA BERETTA
LAURA MAZZETTI
ALBERTO BERNASCONI
ANDREA DE VITTORI
STEFANO ALBERT
MAURIZIO CIVELLI
CECILIA ORTONOVI
LAURA MARTINEZ DEL OLMO
ANDREA GIACOMO MONFRINI
ALBERTO CARILLO
MADDALENA LAZZARI
MATTEO POZZI
MATTEO VALENTE

Former Interns

ANTONIO PULLARA
SOFIA DELL'OCA
RINA SOFTA
DAVIDE FIN
ELIA RUSCONI
EMANUELE CARCANO
MARCO BRIGHENTI
MICHAEL GUSMERINI
SOFIA ALECCI
PRISCILLA MASTINI
GIANMARCO MARINI
ANDREA CAGGIULA
MATTEO MAURO
DAVID STALDER

ISBN: 9788891633590

Printed in September 2020 on the premises of Maggioli S.p.A. - Santarcangelo di Romagna

CREDITS

■ ■ ■ THE PLAN

CEO
PAOLO MAGGIOLI
Maggioli S.p.A.
Via del Carpino, 8 - Santarcangelo di Romagna - Italy

Editor-in-Chief
CARLOTTA ZUCCHINI

Managing Editor
NICOLA LEONARDI

OPEN BEING

A project by
MINO CAGGIULA ARCHITECTS

Consultant
ENRICO LEONARDO FAGONE

Editorial Coordination
FORTESA SOFTA

Editorial Staff
MINO CAGGIULA
ENRICO LEONARDO FAGONE
FORTESA SOFTA
MATTIA SANTI

Graphics and Layout
GIANFRANCO CESARI

Photography
PAOLO VOLONTÈ
MASSIMO PEDRAZZINI
SAMUELE SCHIATTI
SANTI & SANTI

Publisher
Maggioli S.p.A.
Via del Carpino, 8 - Santarcangelo di Romagna
www.maggiolieditore.it - E-mail: clienti.editore@maggioli.it